Grammar Minutes

Written by
Carmen S. Jones

Editor: Maria Elvira Gallardo, MA
Cover Illustrator: Rick Grayson
Cover Designer: Rebekah O. Lewis
Production: Rebekah O. Lewis
Art Director: Moonhee Pak
Project Director: Stacey Faulkner

Table of Contents

Introduction

The main objective of *Grammar Minutes Grade 2* is grammar proficiency, attained by teaching students to apply grammar skills to answer questions effortlessly and rapidly. The questions in this book provide students with practice in the following key areas of second-grade grammar instruction:

- sentence structure
- capital letters
- punctuation
- nouns
- verbs
- pronouns
- adjectives
- adverbs
- contractions
- compound words
- articles

Use this comprehensive resource to improve your students' overall grammar proficiency, which will promote greater self-confidence in their grammar skills as well as provide the everyday practice necessary to succeed in testing situations.

Grammar Minutes Grade 2 features 100 "Minutes." Each Minute consists of 10 questions for students to complete within a short time period. As students are becoming familiar with the format of the Minutes, they may need more time to complete each one. Once they are comfortable and familiar with the format, give students a one- to two-minute period to complete each Minute. The quick, timed format, combined with instant feedback, makes this a challenging and motivational assignment that offers students an ongoing opportunity to improve their own proficiency in a manageable, nonthreatening way.

How to Use This Book

Grammar Minutes Grade 2 is designed to generally progress through the skills as they are introduced in the classroom in second grade. The Minutes can be implemented in either numerical order, starting with Minute 1, or in any order based on your students' specific needs during the school year. The complexity of the sentences and the tasks within each skill being covered gradually increase so that the first Minute of a skill is generally easier than the second Minute on the same skill. Review lessons are included throughout the book, as well as in an application section at the end of the book.

Grammar Minutes Grade 2 can be used in a variety of ways. Use one Minute a day as a warm-up activity, skill review, assessment, test prep, extra credit assignment, or homework assignment. Keep in mind that students will get the most benefit from each Minute if they receive immediate feedback.

If you use the Minute as a timed activity, begin by placing the paper facedown on the students' desks or displaying it as a transparency. Use a clock or kitchen timer to measure one minute—or more if needed. As the Minutes become more advanced, use your discretion on extending the time frame to several minutes if needed. Encourage students to concentrate on completing each question successfully and not to dwell on questions they cannot complete. At the end of the allotted time, have the students stop working. Read the answers from the answer key (pages 108–112) or display them on a transparency. Have students correct their own work and record their scores on the Minute Journal reproducible (page 6). Then have the class go over each question together to discuss the answers. Spend more time on questions that were clearly challenging for most of the class. Tell students that some skills that seemed difficult for them will appear again on future Minutes and that they will have another opportunity for success.

Teach students the following strategies for improving their scores, especially if you time their work on each Minute:

- leave more challenging items for last
- come back to items they are unsure of after they have completed all other items
- make educated guesses when they encounter items with which they are unfamiliar
- ask questions if they are still unsure about anything

Students will ultimately learn to apply these strategies to other assignments and testing situations.

The Minutes are designed to assess and improve grammar proficiency and should not be included as part of a student's overall language arts grade. However, the Minutes provide an excellent opportunity to identify which skills the class as a whole needs to practice or review. Use this information to plan the content of future grammar lessons. For example, if many students in the class have difficulty with a Minute on commas, additional lessons in that area will be useful and valuable for the students' future success.

While Minute scores will not necessarily be included in students' formal grades, it is important to recognize student improvements by offering individual or class rewards and incentives for scores above a certain level on a daily and/or weekly basis. Showing students recognition for their efforts provides additional motivation to succeed.

Minute Journal

Name _____

Minute	Date	Score	Minute	Date	Score	Minute	Date	Score	Minute	Date	Score
1			26			51			76		
2			27			52			77		
3			28			53			78		
4			29			54			79		
5			30			55			80		
6			31			56			81		
7			32			57			82		
8			33			58			83		
9			34			59			84		
10			35			60			85		
11			36			61			86		
12			37			62			87		
13			38			63			88		
14			39			64			89		
15			40			65			90		
16			41			66			91		
17			42			67			92		
18			43			68			93		
19			44			69			94		
20			45			70			95		
21			46			71			96		
22			47			72			97		
23			48			73			98		
24			49			74			99		
25			50			75			100		

Grammar Minutes • Grade 2 © 2009 Creative Teaching Press

Scope and Sequence

Minute 1

Name _____

For Numbers 1–4, circle the sentences that are complete.

1. **a.** The sleeping dog.
   b. The dog takes a short nap.

2. **a.** Kyle helps his dad rake leaves.
   b. In the summer.

3. **a.** The dog looks the bird.
   b. The cat watched the bird in the tree.

4. **a.** Mrs. Clarke was my teacher.
   b. In the backyard.

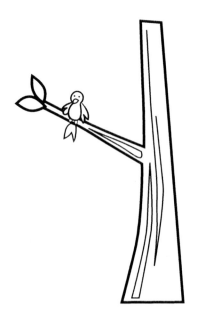

For Numbers 5–10, circle *Complete* if the sentence is complete or *Incomplete* if it is not.

5.	The dog had fun at the park.	Complete	Incomplete
6.	Skate for an hour.	Complete	Incomplete
7.	We had lots of fun too.	Complete	Incomplete
8.	The girls walked to the playground.	Complete	Incomplete
9.	The yellow butterfly.	Complete	Incomplete
10.	The ice cream cone tastes good.	Complete	Incomplete

Grammar Minutes • Grade 2 © 2009 Creative Teaching Press

Minute 2

Name _____

For Numbers 1–5, circle the sentences that are in the correct word order.

1. a. The snake mud slides the through.
    b. The snake slides through the mud.

2. a. The clown makes the children laugh.
    b. The children makes laugh the clown.

3. a. The apples in the tree are rotten.
    b. The tree apples in the are rotten.

4. a. At beach had the fun Regina.
    b. Regina had fun at the beach.

5. a. We went to Florida on vacation.
    b. Florida we went to on vacation.

For Numbers 6–10, rewrite the sentences in the correct word order.

6. Funny movie was the. _____

7. I bike my on ride. _____

8. The sleeps lot a cat. _____

9. Sweet the candy is. _____

10. Was puppy the lost. _____

Grammar Minutes • Grade 2 © 2009 Creative Teaching Press

Sentence Word Order

Minute 3

Name _____

Read each sentence, and write the type of sentence it is on the line. Put *T* for telling, *A* for asking, or *E* for exclaiming.

1. Do you have a pencil? _____

2. There are seven days in a week. _____

3. I can't wait until vacation! _____

4. When is your birthday party? _____

5. My teacher loves green apples. _____

6. Our club is going camping. _____

7. May I make my own lunch today? _____

8. I spilled milk on my dress! _____

9. There are six fish in the pond. _____

10. Tony and Jay play football. _____

Minute 4

Name _____

For Numbers 1–3, circle the correct telling sentences.

1. **a.** May we go to the park.   **b.** We are going to the park.

2. **a.** Bob and John play basketball.   **b.** Wow, Bob made five baskets.

3. **a.** The cat climbs the tree.   **b.** Is your cat in the tree.

For Numbers 4–6, circle the correct asking sentences.

4. **a.** What time are we going to the game?
    b. The pizza tastes so good?

5. **a.** My mother makes the best chocolate cake?
    b. How are you doing today?

6. **a.** Brenda and Carmen love to go shopping?
    b. Why do birds fly south for the winter?

For Numbers 7–10, circle the correct exclaiming sentences.

7. **a.** Chelsea danced in the show!
    b. Wow, Chelsea was great in the show!

8. **a.** You are a terrific dancer!
    b. I have dance class on Saturdays!

9. **a.** The tree is falling down on our house!
    b. We have a tree in front of our house!

10. **a.** A red car is coming up the street!
    b. Watch out for that car!

More on Types of Sentences

Minute 5

Name _____

Circle the word in each sentence that should begin with a capital letter, and write it correctly on the line.

1. i play football every day.   _____

2. we fly kites at Grant Park.   _____

3. sarah's mother makes the best apple pie.   _____

4. wednesday is the day of our math test.   _____

5. my dad was born in New York.   _____

6. april is my favorite month of the year.   _____

7. max is my dog's name.   _____

8. california has a lot of nice beaches.   _____

9. they like to shop at Turner Mall.   _____

10. every Friday we eat pizza for dinner.   _____

Grammar Minutes • Grade 2 © 2009 Creative Teaching Press

Minute 6

Name _____

Add the correct punctuation mark to the end of each sentence.

1. May we have popcorn _____

2. The movie was great _____

3. Sit down now _____

4. The students walked to school _____

5. Sam and Susie baked cookies _____

6. Why do birds fly south for the winter _____

7. Get that away from me _____

8. Martin's dad is a police officer _____

9. The red fish swam in the bay _____

10. When does your party start _____

Grammar Minutes • Grade 2 © 2009 Creative Teaching Press

Ending a Sentence

Minute 7

Name _____

Place each noun (naming word) in the correct box below.

student	phone	park	sister	flower
school	radio	teacher	lake	coach
Person		**Place**		**Thing**

1. _____   5. _____   8. _____

2. _____   6. _____   9. _____

3. _____   7. _____   10. _____

4. _____

Minute 8

Name _____

Circle the nouns (naming words) in the sentences.
(**Hint**: Each sentence has two nouns to circle.)

1. The girls play in the park.

2. Brandon likes to read scary books.

3. Apples and grapes taste good.

4. Marie and Tina are playing.

5. Tom baked a chocolate cake.

6. The beach is fun during the summer.

7. Chris is looking for his dog.

8. The dog chased the cat.

9. The clouds in the sky are fluffy.

10. Mr. Manson is a new teacher.

More Nouns

Minute 9

Name _____

Circle the proper nouns (naming words) that should begin with capital letters in the sentences below.

(**Hint**: *Proper nouns* name specific people, places, things, or animals.)

1. meg and amy are sisters.

2. My dog charlie is gray and white.

3. I asked nick and mitch to help me.

4. The cat's name is lucky.

5. We named the rabbit in our class punka.

6. Our class saw timothy the tiger at the zoo.

7. The teacher's helper is nicole.

8. megan and madison are twins.

9. I have a bird named mozart.

10. She brought her hamster bubbles to school.

Grammar Minutes • Grade 2 © 2009 Creative Teaching Press

Minute 10

Name _____

Circle the correct way to write the days of the week and months of the year.

1. a. friday
    b. Friday

2. a. December
    b. december

3. a. august
    b. August

4. a. Monday
    b. monday

5. a. sunday
    b. Sunday

6. a. March
    b. march

7. a. may
    b. May

8. a. Wednesday
    b. wednesday

9. a. Tuesday
    b. tuesday

10. a. september
    b. September

Grammar Minutes • Grade 2 © 2009 Creative Teaching Press

Proper Nouns (days and months)

Minute 11

Name _____

For Numbers 1–5, circle the proper nouns for people in the sentences.

1. Uncle Herbert cut down the tree.

2. My dentist is Dr. Dawson.

3. The students like Mrs. Gomez.

4. Police Officer Edwards spoke to our class.

5. I baked apple pies with Grandma Rose.

For Numbers 6–10, circle the correct way to write each name.

6. **a.** dr. allen   **b.** Dr. allen   **c.** Dr. Allen

7. **a.** Coach Simmons   **b.** coach Simmons   **c.** Coach simmons

8. **a.** uncle Mike   **b.** Uncle Mike   **c.** Uncle mike

9. **a.** Ms. patrick   **b.** ms. Patrick   **c.** Ms. Patrick

10. **a.** Principal jones   **b.** Principal Jones   **c.** principal jones

Grammar Minutes • Grade 2 © 2009 Creative Teaching Press

Minute 12

Name _____

Circle the proper nouns for places in the sentences.

1. I went to Washington Elementary School.

2. We saw flowers at Parker Garden Center.

3. Burger Express is my favorite place to eat.

4. My sister works at Doggie Kennel.

5. She is from Chicago, Illinois.

6. We had so much fun at Rose Park.

7. Bouldercrest Mall has lots of stores.

8. Florida has the best beaches.

9. I have a library card for Smith Library.

10. The girls live on Jackson Street.

Proper Nouns (places)

Minute 13

Name _____

For Numbers 1–3, write *C* on the line if the sentence is complete or *I* if it is incomplete.

1. We had pizza for dinner on Friday. _____

2. The cute little baby. _____

3. Larry and Barry are singing a song. _____

For Numbers 4–5, circle the sentences that are in the correct word order.

4. **a.** Ralph is going to the basketball game.
    b. Going to the Ralph is basketball game.

5. **a.** The flowers in her garden likes to water my mother.
    b. My mother likes to water the flowers in her garden.

For Numbers 6–10, read each sentence and write the type of sentence it is on the line. Put *T* for telling, *A* for asking, or *E* for exclaiming.

6. I love going to ballet class. _____

7. I almost fell off of the stage! _____

8. When are you coming to watch me dance? _____

9. Watch out for the big bug! _____

10. Why do the clouds look white? _____

Grammar Minutes • Grade 2 © 2009 Creative Teaching Press

Minute 14

Name _____

For Numbers 1–5, rewrite each sentence correctly on the line.

1. how are you? _____

2. my desk is dirty. _____

3. the clock is black. _____

4. wow, she's tall! _____

5. i play the piano. _____

For Numbers 6–10, circle *Yes* if the sentence ends with the correct punctuation mark or *No* if it does not.

6. Wow, I just won a new bike.   Yes   No

7. How are Tom and Susie doing.   Yes   No

8. We are taking class pictures on Friday.   Yes   No

9. On what day do we have music class?   Yes   No

10. Scott's birthday is on Saturday!   Yes   No

Minute 15

Name _____

For Numbers 1–6, write each noun in the correct box below.

bedroom ring	singer principal	hospital brush
Person	**Place**	**Thing**
1. _____	3. _____	5. _____
2. _____	4. _____	6. _____

For Numbers 7–10, circle the nouns in the sentences.
(**Hint**: Each sentence has two nouns to circle.)

7. The firefighter saved the kitten.

8. There are flowers in the garden.

9. The dog tore up his toy.

10. The nurse took care of my cut.

Grammar Minutes • Grade 2 © 2009 Creative Teaching Press

Minute 16

Name _____

Circle the proper nouns that are missing their capital letters in the sentences below.

1. Mr. thomas is my second-grade teacher.

2. I go to lincoln Elementary School.

3. Mr. Thomas is from seattle, Washington.

4. He went to the University of washington.

5. Today our class is going to the atlanta Zoo.

6. johnny's mom is going to help Mr. Thomas.

7. Principal greene is going with us as well.

8. We will get to see chi, the famous panda bear.

9. I hope the other panda bear, hua, is there too.

10. My best friend, jennifer, and I can't wait to go!

Grammar Minutes • Grade 2 © 2009 Creative Teaching Press

Proper Nouns Review

Minute 17

Name _____

Circle the 10 verbs (action words) in the box below.

chew	dance	jump
pretty	teacher	big
swim	smell	song
puppy	pizza	eraser
clap	walk	drive
red	pillow	hat
computer	paper	kite
type	eat	spider

Grammar Minutes • Grade 2 © 2009 Creative Teaching Press

Minute 18

Name _____

Circle the verb in each sentence.

1. The girl feeds the ducks.

2. The dog barks at the cat.

3. The boys play football.

4. The mother reads a book to her son.

5. I walked around the park.

6. We swam every day in June.

7. The snail slides on the ground.

8. Bobby and Cindy rode their bikes.

9. The birds chirp in the tree.

10. Debbie types on the computer.

More Verbs

Minute 19

Name _____

Circle the correct verb in each sentence.

1. We (jogs, jogged) at the park yesterday.

2. The boys (play, played) basketball last night.

3. Mrs. Clarke (helps, helped) us every day.

4. Right now I (have, had) long hair.

5. My brother (is, was) at camp last week.

6. Lisa (dances, danced) in the show two years ago.

7. The baby (cries, cried) all last night.

8. My new dog (licks, licked) me when I have food.

9. The principal (pulls, pulled) the flag up every morning.

10. The bus driver (chews, chewed) gum all the time.

Minute 20

Name _____

For Numbers 1–6, write the correct verb in each sentence.

(**Hint**: When something happens now, it is *present tense*. When something happened already, it is *past tense*.)

Present Tense	Past Tense
1. The dog _____ scratches scratched himself.	**2.** I _____ scratches scratched my itchy arm.
3. I _____ when yawned yawn I am sleepy.	**4.** She _____ yawned yawn all morning.
5. We _____ with write wrote pink pens.	**6.** My friends _____ a poem. write wrote

For Numbers 7–10, circle the correct verb in each sentence.

7. My birthday (is, was) later this month.

8. He (rakes, raked) the leaves yesterday.

9. Sunflowers (look, looked) pretty when they grow tall.

10. Sammy (pitches, pitched) in last week's game.

Grammar Minutes • Grade 2 © 2009 Creative Teaching Press

More on Verb Tense

Minute 21

Name _____

Circle the correct verb (*is, are,* or *am*) in each sentence.

1. My name (is, are, am) Johnny.

2. The leaves (is, are, am) yellow.

3. I (is, are, am) the star of the play.

4. The dog (is, are, am) well trained.

5. My dad (is, are, am) the president of his company.

6. My family (is, are, am) at the baseball game.

7. A lion (is, are, am) a strong animal.

8. I (is, are, am) afraid of the dark.

9. There (is, are, am) five birds in the cage.

10. The flower garden (is, are, am) colorful.

Grammar Minutes • Grade 2 © 2009 Creative Teaching Press

Minute 22

Name _____

Circle the correct verb (*was* or *were*) in each sentence.

1. The cow (was, were) on the grass.

2. The sun (was, were) so hot, the plants died.

3. The children (was, were) excited about the party.

4. The book (was, were) under the desk.

5. Our costumes (was, were) the best ones.

6. Kathy (was, were) asleep all day!

7. The dolphins (was, were) fun to watch.

8. The cake (was, were) yummy!

9. The streets (was, were) wet from the rain.

10. The spider (was, were) on the window.

Grammar Minutes • Grade 2 © 2009 Creative Teaching Press

Linking Verbs (was, were)

Minute 23

Name _____

Circle the correct verb (*have, has,* or *had*) in each sentence.

1. We now (have, has, had) three computers in our classroom.

2. The teacher also (have, has, had) her own computer now.

3. Joey and Sam (have, has, had) the same lunch today.

4. Sarah and Perry (have, has, had) a test tomorrow.

5. Our teacher (have, has, had) a little dog.

6. These trees always (have, has, had) lots of leaves.

7. My cousin (have, has, had) a cold right now.

8. We (have, has, had) pizza for lunch yesterday.

9. Rick and Larry (have, has, had) fun last summer.

10. The cookies I am making (have, has, had) nuts in them.

Grammar Minutes • Grade 2 © 2009 Creative Teaching Press

Minute 24

Name _____

Circle the adjective (describing word) in each sentence.

(**Hint**: Each sentence has one adjective to circle.)

1. The gray puppy licked his paws.

2. The strawberries are sweet.

3. There are five birds in the sky.

4. Kim drew a pretty picture of a rainbow.

5. I tasted the sour lemon.

6. The tiny mouse ran into the hole.

7. My father likes green apples.

8. The loud music hurts my ears.

9. The cat was chased by a mean dog.

10. The little girl's hamster died.

Grammar Minutes • Grade 2 © 2009 Creative Teaching Press

Adjectives

Minute 25

Name _____

Circle the correct adjective in each sentence.

(**Hint**: Adjectives that end in *-er* compare two things, and adjectives that end in *-est* compare more than two things.)

1. Mike is (taller, tallest) than Pat.

2. Elaine is the (faster, fastest) painter in art class.

3. Lewis is the (slower, slowest) person of all.

4. Flowers are (shorter, shortest) than trees.

5. The sun is (brighter, brightest) than the moon.

6. John is the (smarter, smartest) boy in school.

7. Laura is the (nicer, nicest) girl I know.

8. Cheetahs are (bigger, biggest) than house cats.

9. The plate is (cleaner, cleanest) than the bowl.

10. He dug the (deeper, deepest) hole he could.

Grammar Minutes • Grade 2 © 2009 Creative Teaching Press

Minute 26

Name _____

For Numbers 1–5, insert the missing comma in each address or place.

1. Wendy lives at 2356 Well Road, Glendale Arizona.

2. I was born in Columbus Ohio.

3. Last summer, Tony went to Paris France.

4. Her party is at 1908 Ivy Lane Washington, D.C.

5. My address is 1152 Peachtree Street Ashton, Idaho.

For Numbers 6–10, insert the missing comma in each date.

6. Judy was born on June 30 1987.

7. Today's date is Wednesday, August 1 2009.

8. The first day of school is on Monday August 13, 2009.

9. My sister starts high school on June 30 2010.

10. My party was on Thursday, May 10 2008.

Commas (addresses and dates)

Grammar Minutes • Grade 2 © 2009 Creative Teaching Press

Minute 27

Name _____

For Numbers 1–4, insert the missing comma in each sentence.

1. I like to read skate, and dance.

2. My brother plays football, soccer and baseball.

3. Sasha ate a hot dog, candy popcorn, and ice cream.

4. Diego saw lions tigers, monkeys, and snakes at the zoo.

For Numbers 5–10, circle the sentences that use the commas correctly.

5. **a.** Carolyn likes, apples oranges, and pears.
b. Carolyn likes apples, oranges, and pears.

6. **a.** I went to the beach, the park, and the zoo.
b. I went to the beach, the park and the zoo.

7. **a.** The teacher gave us scissors glue and crayons.
b. The teacher gave us scissors, glue, and crayons.

8. **a.** We have two birds, a turtle and, a hamster.
b. We have two birds, a turtle, and a hamster.

9. **a.** The flowers are red, yellow, and white.
b. Our school colors are red yellow and, white.

10. **a.** The farm has, chickens, cows ducks and pigs.
b. Thomas has chickens, cows, ducks, and pigs.

Grammar Minutes • Grade 2 © 2009 Creative Teaching Press

Minute 28

Name _____

Read the story and circle the 10 verbs.

Mike's class went on a field trip to the history museum last Friday. He saw

a large display of dinosaurs, and he drew one of the dinosaurs in his

notebook. The teacher told the class to not run or play in the museum. After

the museum tour, the class ate lunch at the park. After lunch, the class rode

back to school on the bus. The next day, the students had to write a story

about their trip and read it to the class.

Grammar Minutes • Grade 2 © 2009 Creative Teaching Press

Verbs Review

Minute 29

Name _____

For Numbers 1–3, write *Yes* if the underlined word is a verb or *No* if it is not.

1. Please give this <u>note</u> to your teacher.   _____

2. Simon <u>bumped</u> his head on the wall.   _____

3. My ears hurt from the <u>loud</u> music.   _____

For Numbers 4–7, circle *Present* if the sentence is in the present tense or *Past* if it is in the past tense.

4. The little boy read 20 books last summer.   Present   Past

5. The children are in the swimming pool.   Present   Past

6. Tom is the class president this year.   Present   Past

7. John and Tim were friends in kindergarten.   Present   Past

For Numbers 8–10, circle the correct verb in each sentence.

8. Yesterday (was, were) Dorian's birthday.

9. Martin (is, are, am) on the basketball team.

10. My dog Lucy (have, has, had) her puppies last month.

More Verbs Review

Grammar Minutes • Grade 2 © 2009 Creative Teaching Press

Minute 30

Name _____

For Numbers 1–4, use an adjective from the box to complete each sentence.

| red | fresh | fastest | smart |

1. Sherry and Mandy are _____ students.

2. Angela is the _____ runner on her team.

3. The shiny _____ car had a flat tire.

4. The mouse found a _____ piece of cheese.

For Numbers 5–7, circle the adjective in each sentence.

5. The yellow roses grow in the spring.

6. Tonya put roses in her prettiest vase.

7. The roses made a beautiful gift for her mother.

For Numbers 8–10, circle the correct adjective in each sentence.

8. Apples are (healthy, healthier, healthiest) than candy.

9. Regina's poem was the (good, better, best) one of all.

10. A watermelon is much (long, longer, longest) than a banana.

Adjectives Review

Minute 31

Name _____

For Numbers 1–3, insert the missing comma in each sentence.

1. I like to eat pancakes eggs, and bacon for breakfast.

2. My address is 3456 Sanchez Way, Austin Texas.

3. We saw fireworks on July 4 2008.

For Numbers 4–6, circle the sentences that use the commas correctly.

4. a. We ate popcorn, nachos and hot dogs, at the fair.
b. We ate popcorn, nachos, and hot dogs at the fair.

5. a. Kelly was born on January 20, 1995.
b. Kelly was born on January, 20 1995.

6. a. We live in Atlanta Georgia.
b. We live in Atlanta, Georgia.

For Numbers 7–10, write *Yes* if the commas are used correctly or *No* if they are not.

7. The play was on Wednesday, February, 12 2005. _____

8. My grandma lives in Mexico City, Mexico. _____

9. My favorite fruits are oranges, cherries, and grapes. _____

10. His address is 323 Jones Way, Springfield Kansas. _____

Grammar Minutes • Grade 2 © 2009 Creative Teaching Press

Minute 32

Name _____

Circle the correct pronoun in each sentence.

1. (I, Me) love to drink chocolate milk.

2. Is the bus picking (I, me) up for school?

3. The water splashed on (I, me).

4. (I, Me) play the drums in the band.

5. Julio stands behind (I, me) in line.

6. The two turtles belong to (I, me).

7. (I, Me) visit my grandparents every Sunday.

8. Why do (I, me) have to go to the doctor?

9. The lions and the tigers scare (I, me).

10. The monkeys are looking at (I, me).

Pronouns (I, me)

Minute 33

Name _____

For Numbers 1–5, write *Yes* if the underlined pronoun is used correctly or *No* if it is not.

1. <u>Him</u> watches the football game with his dad. _____

2. Dad is getting <u>her</u> a pony. _____

3. I gave <u>he</u> the directions to my house. _____

4. <u>Him</u> had the flu for two weeks! _____

5. <u>She</u> makes dinner every night. _____

For Numbers 6–10, circle the pronoun that could take the place of the underlined noun.

6. <u>Benson</u> has five dollars in the bank. He Him

7. <u>Maria</u> likes the color pink. She Her

8. Tom plays tennis with <u>Meg</u>. she her

9. The teacher asked <u>Doug</u> for the answer. he him

10. <u>Kelly</u> caught more fish at the lake. She Her

Minute 34

Name _____

Circle the correct pronoun in each sentence.

1. (We, Us) are going to the pet store.

2. My best friend is going with (we, us).

3. (We, Us) can get a hamster at the pet store.

4. I hope that the hamster likes (we, us).

5. (We, Us) are going to name him Harvey.

6. (We, Us) stay up late on the weekends.

7. Our mother tells (we, us) to do our homework.

8. Sometimes (we, us) eat cake and ice cream for dessert.

9. (We, Us) always brush our teeth after dinner.

10. My dad reads (we, us) a bedtime story every night.

Pronouns (we, us)

Minute 35

Name _____

For Numbers 1–5, write the pronoun *they* or *them* on the line to take the place of the underlined words in each sentence.
(**Hint**: Remember that a sentence must begin with a capital letter.)

1. The turtles like to eat lettuce.   _____

2. We are waiting for Helen and Jen.   _____

3. The Kesslers are moving to New York.   _____

4. Sam and Jason are going with us to the beach.   _____

5. Do we have to take Sue and Jon with us?   _____

For Numbers 6–10, write *Yes* if the underlined pronoun is used correctly or *No* if it is not.

6. Them are both my best friends.   _____

7. We should invite them to play tag.   _____

8. My parents were happy when they
saw my grades.   _____

9. The candies are so good, I could eat
them all!   _____

10. Them are the best dancers in the show.   _____

Grammar Minutes • Grade 2 © 2009 Creative Teaching Press

Minute 36

Name _____

For Numbers 1–6, circle the noun that is plural in each sentence.
(Hint: *Plural* means more than one.)

1. My sister does not like to wear dresses.

2. Spot chases the cats in the neighborhood.

3. The two girls always play ball at recess.

4. I went to many beaches this summer.

5. The foxes ran quickly around the field.

6. The ponies were so fun to ride.

For Numbers 7–10, circle the correct plural noun in each sentence.

7. I have two best (friends, friendes) at school.

8. Susie got lots of (toys, toies) for her birthday.

9. Tony and his (brotheres, brothers) like soccer.

10. California has many (cities, citys) by the beach.

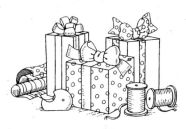

Grammar Minutes • Grade 2 © 2009 Creative Teaching Press

Plural Nouns

Minute 37

Name _____

For Numbers 1–5, circle the plural noun that is spelled correctly in each pair.

1. ponies   ponys

2. babys   babies

3. truckies   trucks

4. foxes   foxs

5. glassies   glasses

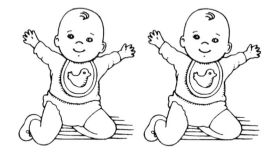

For Numbers 6–10, write each noun in plural form.
(**Hint**: Add *-s* or *-es* to the end of each noun.)

6. pencil   _____

7. apple   _____

8. box   _____

9. boy   _____

10. class   _____

Grammar Minutes • Grade 2 © 2009 Creative Teaching Press

Minute 38

Name _____

For Numbers 1–5, add an apostrophe and s ('s) to the underlined nouns to make them possessive.
(Hint: *Possessive nouns* show ownership by a person, place, or thing.)

1. The <u>baby</u> rattle was on the floor.   _____

2. <u>Nicole</u> dress is pink and white.   _____

3. The <u>painter</u> lunchtime is now.   _____

4. The <u>clock</u> battery stopped working.   _____

5. The <u>city</u> lights are bright at night.   _____

For Numbers 6–8, circle the correct possessive form for each group of words in bold.

6. **neck of a giraffe**   a neck's giraffe   a giraffe's neck

7. **mat that belongs to the dog**   the dog's mat   the mat's dog

8. **shell of the turtle**   the turtle's shell   the shell's turtle

For Numbers 9–10, rewrite each group of words to make them possessive.

9. tires of the car   _____

10. dress that belongs to Ming   _____

Possessive Nouns

Minute 39

Name _____

For **Numbers 1–5**, circle the contraction in each sentence.

1. Don't walk in the middle of the street!

2. I'm going to the pet store to buy a turtle.

3. The little boy can't reach the cookie jar.

4. I haven't read that book yet.

5. We shouldn't be mean to the new student.

For **Numbers 6–10**, write *Yes* if the contraction is spelled correctly or *No* if it is not.

6. was'nt _____

7. he's _____

8. couldn' _____

9. it's _____

10. I'm _____

Grammar Minutes • Grade 2 © 2009 Creative Teaching Press

Minute 40

Name _____

For Numbers 1–5, write the contractions for the underlined words.

1. I <u>have not</u> finished my homework.   _____

2. The puppy <u>was not</u> scared of the big dog.   _____

3. <u>She is</u> very happy to see you.   _____

4. <u>I will</u> buy a pencil at school.   _____

5. I <u>did not</u> finish the math test.   _____

For Numbers 6–10, circle the correct two words that make up each contraction in bold.

6. can't   can not   could not

7. isn't   am not   is not

8. don't   did not   do not

9. hasn't   has not   have not

10. shouldn't   shall not   should not

Grammar Minutes • Grade 2 © 2009 Creative Teaching Press

More Contractions

Minute 41

Name _____

For Numbers 1–4, use the two words to make a compound word.

1. dog   house   _____

2. coat   rain   _____

3. sun   glasses   _____

4. paper   news   _____

For Numbers 5–10, make compound words using the words in the box below. Use each word only once.

after	father	noon	water
tooth	paste	home	grand
melon	room	class	work

5. _____

6. _____

7. _____

8. _____

9. _____

10. _____

Grammar Minutes • Grade 2 © 2009 Creative Teaching Press

Minute 42

Name _____

For Numbers 1–4, circle the compound word in each sentence.

1. The twins play in the backyard.

2. Please go outside and wash the dog.

3. We are riding our bikes to the playground.

4. Eric and Tony play basketball on the same team.

For Numbers 5–10, write *Yes* if the word is a compound word or *No* if it is not.

5. sunshine _____

6. television _____

7. calendar _____

8. upstairs _____

9. background _____

10. computer _____

Grammar Minutes • Grade 2 © 2009 Creative Teaching Press

More Compound Words

Minute 43

Name _____

For Numbers 1–5, replace the underlined noun or nouns with a pronoun.

1. <u>Karen</u> missed school all week.   _____

2. <u>Dan and Jim</u> went to the movies.   _____

3. Mike gave <u>Mark</u> a birthday card.   _____

4. <u>Bob</u> broke his computer again.   _____

5. <u>Dorothy</u> can speak Spanish very well.   _____

For Numbers 6–10, circle the correct pronoun in each sentence.

6. Our teacher played soccer with (we, us) today.

7. (He, Him) wants to become a doctor.

8. (They, Them) are having a party next Saturday.

9. Marcy didn't tell (she, her) the truth.

10. (I, Me) can meet you at the library later.

Grammar Minutes • Grade 2 © 2009 Creative Teaching Press

Minute 44

Name _____

For Numbers 1–5, write the nouns in plural form.

1. carrot _____

2. family _____

3. couch _____

4. class _____

5. ax _____

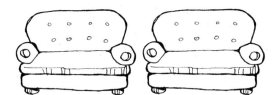

For Numbers 6–10, circle the possessive noun in each sentence.

6. My (dog's, dogs) tail wags fast.

7. The (cakes, cake's) frosting is vanilla.

8. The (children, children's) bikes are in the garage.

9. That (chair's, chairs) leg is broken.

10. His (computers, computer's) screen is dirty.

Plural and Possessive Nouns Review

Minute 45

Name _____

For Numbers 1–5, write the contraction for the two words.

1. he is _____

2. does not _____

3. are not _____

4. you are _____

5. you will _____

For Numbers 6–10, write the two words that make up each contraction.

6. would've _____ _____

7. won't _____ _____

8. isn't _____ _____

9. didn't _____ _____

10. mustn't _____ _____

Grammar Minutes • Grade 2 © 2009 Creative Teaching Press

Minute 46

Name _____

Circle the compound word in each sentence.

1. We saw skyscrapers in New York City.

2. The earthworm crawled through the dirt.

3. Do you have any peppermints?

4. We built a snowman after the storm.

5. My wristwatch stopped working.

6. The sunflowers grew as tall as I am.

7. My dad built a birdhouse for my garden.

8. Julie sent me a postcard from her vacation.

9. Jake was scared of the rattlesnake at the zoo.

10. Katie forgot to do her homework.

Compound Words Review

Minute 47

Name _____

For Numbers 1–6, write the best synonym for each word.
(**Hint**: A *synonym* is a word that means the same thing or almost the same thing.)

| beautiful | small | scream | angry | sleepy | hop |

1. mad _____

2. yell _____

3. pretty _____

4. skip _____

5. tired _____

6. tiny _____

For Numbers 7–10, circle the synonym for each underlined word.

7. Angel <u>dislikes</u> cats. hates loves

8. My <u>friend</u> George is funny. buddy girl

9. Tosha was <u>sad</u> when her fish died. happy unhappy

10. I <u>finished</u> my homework already. completed started

Grammar Minutes • Grade 2 © 2009 Creative Teaching Press

Minute 48

Name _____

For Numbers 1–4, circle the two synonyms in each group of words.

1. quiet   noisy   silent   bark

2. old   new   ancient   dull

3. yell   talk   speak   walk

4. rich   poor   wealthy   nice

For Numbers 5–10, write *Yes* if the pairs of words are synonyms or *No* if they are not.

5. run   walk   _____

6. cook   eat   _____

7. cry   smile   _____

8. sleep   awake   _____

9. jump   hop   _____

10. draw   illustrate   _____

Grammar Minutes • Grade 2 © 2009 Creative Teaching Press

More Synonyms

Minute 49

Name _____

For Numbers 1–6, write the best antonym for each word.

(**Hint**: An *antonym* is a word that means the opposite of something.)

sit	forget	run
asleep	up	go

1. stop   _____

2. down   _____

3. stand   _____

4. awake   _____

5. remember   _____

6. walk   _____

For Numbers 7–10, circle the antonym for each underlined word.

7. The diamond ring is <u>shiny</u>.   dull   bright

8. The music was <u>noisy</u>.   loud   quiet

9. The <u>little</u> dog ran to his owner.   huge   tiny

10. My mother said to clean my <u>dirty</u> room.   neat   filthy

Grammar Minutes • Grade 2 © 2009 Creative Teaching Press

Minute 50

Name _____

For Numbers 1–6, circle the antonym for each word in bold.

1. early   on time   late

2. cold   frozen   hot

3. left   right   wrong

4. good   super   terrible

5. wet   dry   damp

6. ugly   pretty   strong

For Numbers 7–10, complete each sentence with an antonym for the underlined word.

7. The swing went up and _____.

8. My brother is a slow runner, but I am a _____ runner.

9. I don't like big dogs. I like _____ dogs.

10. The bird flew high in the sky, then _____ to the ground.

Grammar Minutes • Grade 2 © 2009 Creative Teaching Press

More Antonyms

Minute 51

Name _____

For Numbers 1–6, circle the correct homophone in each sentence.
(**Hint**: *Homophones* are words that sound the same but are spelled differently and have different meanings.)

1. The (sun, son) is shining brightly in the sky.

2. We can (see, sea) the top of the mountain from here.

3. May I please have a (piece, peace) of cake?

4. The hawk watches his (prey, pray) from the tree.

5. A (be, bee) in my garden stung me on my arm.

6. My favorite color is sky (blew, blue).

For Numbers 7–10, write *Yes* if the words are homophones or *No* if they are not.

7. right   write   _____

8. dig   bury   _____

9. to   too   _____

10. small   little   _____

Grammar Minutes • Grade 2 © 2009 Creative Teaching Press

Minute 52

Name _____

For Numbers 1–6, circle the correct meaning for the underlined homograph in each sentence.

(**Hint**: *Homographs* are words that are spelled the same—and sometimes sound the same—but have different meanings.)

1. Be careful not to <u>break</u> anything!
   a. a rest
   b. to smash

2. He hit the ball hard with the <u>bat</u>.
   a. a piece of wood or metal
   b. a flying mammal

3. The <u>wind</u> blew my hat off.
   a. to turn
   b. a strong current of air

4. The <u>bug</u> crawled up his leg.
   a. to bother
   b. an insect

5. Put the water in a big <u>pitcher</u>.
   a. a jug
   b. a baseball player

6. You should never <u>lie</u> to your parents.
   a. to rest down flat
   b. to speak untruthfully

For Numbers 7–10, draw a line to match the underlined homograph in each sentence with its correct meaning.

7. Please <u>bow</u> when the Queen walks in.

8. She had a beautiful <u>bow</u> in her hair.

9. I will <u>plant</u> some roses today.

10. The <u>plant</u> grew very tall.

a. a living thing with leaves

b. to put something in the ground

c. to bend down from the waist

d. a knotted ribbon

Homographs

Minute 53

Name _____

For Numbers 1–5, add the prefix *re-* or *un-* to the beginning of the underlined word in each sentence. Use the information in the box about prefixes to help you.

(**Hint**: A *prefix* changes the meaning of a word by adding a group of letters to the beginning of a word.)

Prefix	Meaning	Example
re-	again; back	<u>re</u>do (do again)
un-	not; opposite	<u>un</u>clean (not clean)

1. Yesterday Mrs. Chen was <u>happy</u>, but today she is _____.

2. I <u>write</u> my homework quickly, and then I _____ it.

3. Don't eat an _____ snack if you could eat a <u>healthy</u> one instead.

4. <u>Fill</u> the glasses with water, and be sure to _____ them when they get empty.

5. I got really <u>lucky</u> today, but I was _____ yesterday.

For Numbers 6–10, draw a line to match the underlined word in each sentence with its correct definition.

6. Her birthday gifts are still <u>unwrapped</u>.   **a.** not clear

7. My dress was still dirty, so I <u>rewashed</u> it.   **b.** wrapped again

8. The directions for the test were <u>unclear</u>.   **c.** not wrapped

9. Please <u>redraw</u> that messy illustration.   **d.** washed again

10. Susie <u>rewrapped</u> the gifts after she peeked at them.   **e.** draw again

Grammar Minutes • Grade 2 © 2009 Creative Teaching Press

Minute 54

Name _____

For Numbers 1–5, use the information in the box about suffixes to write the word that best completes each sentence.

(**Hint**: A *suffix* changes the meaning of a word by adding a group of letters to the end of a word.)

Suffix	Meaning	Example
-er	one who; a person who	singer (a person who sings)
-ful	full of	painful (full of pain)

1. The teacher said that Johnny is a good _____.

helpful   helper

2. Miguel's mean words were _____ to me.

hurter   hurtful

3. Tonya is the best _____ on their team.

playful   player

4. The teacher thinks Holly is a _____ student.

helpful   helper

5. The monkeys at the zoo are _____ all day.

playful   player

For Numbers 6–10, underline the word that ends with a suffix in each sentence, and write its meaning on the line.

6. Diego was a famous painter.   _____

7. The walls are bright and colorful.   _____

8. Everyone was cheerful at the party.   _____

9. Omar wants to be a teacher.   _____

10. Ben is hopeful about his grades.   _____

Grammar Minutes • Grade 2 © 2009 Creative Teaching Press

Suffixes

Minute 55

Name _____

For Numbers 1–6, write the words in the box in ABC order.

duck	weather	five
skate	job	grapes

1. _____

2. _____

3. _____

4. _____

5. _____

6. _____

For Numbers 7–10, write *Yes* if the groups of words are in ABC order or *No* if they are not.

7. king   prince   queen   _____

8. book   library   magazine   _____

9. sing   dance   act   _____

10. black   brown   red   _____

Grammar Minutes • Grade 2 © 2009 Creative Teaching Press

Minute 56

Name _____

For Numbers 1–4, write each set of words in ABC order.

1. snap, shake, slide _____

2. apple, any, already _____

3. grape, great, grew _____

4. drum, drink, draw _____

For Numbers 5–10, write the words in the box in ABC order.

house	head	hum
heat	home	handsome

5. _____

6. _____

7. _____

8. _____

9. _____

10. _____

Grammar Minutes • Grade 2 © 2009 Creative Teaching Press

More ABC Order

Minute 57

Name _____

Write *S* if the pairs of words are synonyms (mean the same thing) or *A* if they are antonyms (mean the opposite).

1. neat   clean   _____

2. ugly   pretty   _____

3. high   low   _____

4. lost   missing   _____

5. good   bad   _____

6. happy   cheerful   _____

7. sick   well   _____

8. large   huge   _____

9. hard   easy   _____

10. nice   sweet   _____

Grammar Minutes • Grade 2 © 2009 Creative Teaching Press

Minute 58

Name _____

For Numbers 1–6, write a homophone for each word.

(**Hint:** Remember that *homophones* are words that sound the same but are spelled differently and have different meanings.)

1. son _____

2. maid _____

3. plain _____

4. meat _____

5. right _____

6. high _____

For Numbers 7–10, draw a line to match the underlined homograph in each sentence with its correct meaning.

(**Hint:** Remember that *homographs* are words that are spelled the same—and sometimes sound the same—but have different meanings.)

7. That <u>duck</u> quacks all day and night!

a. to bend down quickly

8. He had to <u>duck</u> so the ball didn't hit him.

b. a built-in bowl with faucets

9. The heavy rock will <u>sink</u> in the water.

c. a waterbird with a wide beak

10. Our kitchen <u>sink</u> is full of dishes.

d. to go down below

Grammar Minutes • Grade 2 © 2009 Creative Teaching Press

Homophones and Homographs Review

Minute 59

Name _____

For Numbers 1–5, write *P* if the underlined word begins with a prefix or *S* if it ends with a suffix.

1. The old glue stick was so dry, it was <u>useless</u>.   _____

2. Please <u>reorder</u> more paper for the office.   _____

3. I am so <u>thankful</u> for all of your help!   _____

4. Charlie banged on our door very <u>loudly</u>.   _____

5. Do not <u>unlock</u> the door for a stranger.   _____

For Numbers 6–10, use a word from the box to complete each sentence.

unpack	reread	replay
driver	beautiful	

6. When the video game ends, I _____ it from the beginning.

7. It is dangerous to be a race car _____.

8. We _____ our clothes in the hotel room.

9. The rainbow in the sky was _____.

10. I have to _____ the book before the test.

Grammar Minutes • Grade 2 © 2009 Creative Teaching Press

Minute 60

Name _____

Write *Yes* if the words are in ABC order or *No* if they are not.

1. sofa, table, chair   _____

2. dirt, rock, water   _____

3. bowl, cup, plate   _____

4. bear, monkey, lion   _____

5. cereal, fruit, meat   _____

6. water, milk, juice   _____

7. bush, flower, plants   _____

8. cook, doctor, nurse   _____

9. rest, socks, shoes   _____

10. cloud, moon, star   _____

Grammar Minutes • Grade 2 © 2009 Creative Teaching Press

ABC Order Review

Minute 61

Name _____

For Numbers 1–4, circle the correct article (*a* or *an*) in each sentence.
(**Hint**: Use *a* before words that begin with a consonant sound, and use *an* before words that begin with a vowel sound.)

1. I have (a, an) ant farm at home.

2. Our school has (a, an) big library.

3. I am getting (a, an) new pair of shoes.

4. (A, An) apple is a healthy snack.

For Numbers 5–10, write the correct article (*a* or *an*) that goes before each word.

5. _____ telephone

6. _____ man

7. _____ egg

8. _____ nose

9. _____ iron

10. _____ teacher

Minute 62

Name _____

Complete each sentence with the missing article *a*, *an*, or *the*.
(**Hint**: Use ***the*** before a word that stands for a specific person, place, or thing. You can use ***the*** before a word that begins with a consonant or a vowel.)

1. My class is going to _____ city zoo this year.

2. I won _____ ribbon at the spelling bee.

3. _____ first-grade classes put on a play.

4. I want _____ ice-cream cone.

5. Our teacher took _____ picture of us at the zoo.

6. She is _____ smartest student in class.

7. I got _____ new bike for my birthday.

8. We went to _____ dentist for a checkup.

9. Have you met _____ new neighbors?

10. _____ orange tastes better than an apple.

More Articles (a, an, the)

Minute 63

Name _____

For Numbers 1–4, circle the correct past-tense verb in each sentence.
(**Hint:** *Past tense* means that something happened already.)

1. I (feeded, fed) my dog twice yesterday.

2. Marcus (throwed, threw) the ball to his father.

3. The children (writed, wrote) a class play.

4. We (maked, made) cookies for the club's bake sale.

For Numbers 5–10, circle each verb in its correct past-tense form.

5. take   took   taked

6. run   runned   ran

7. freeze   freezed   froze

8. stand   stood   standed

9. leave   leaved   left

10. read   readed   read

Grammar Minutes • Grade 2 © 2009 Creative Teaching Press

Minute 64

Name _____

For **Numbers 1–6**, write each verb from the box next to its correct past-tense form.

fight	catch	wear
hold	take	run

1. held   _____

2. took   _____

3. caught   _____

4. fought   _____

5. wore   _____

6. ran   _____

For **Numbers 7–10**, circle the correct verb in each sentence.

7. My mother (taked, took) the dog to the vet.

8. The flowers (growed, grew) in April.

9. The children (swimmed, swam) in the pool all summer.

10. I (selled, sold) lemonade last Saturday.

Grammar Minutes • Grade 2 © 2009 Creative Teaching Press

More Irregular Verbs

Minute 65

Name _____

For Numbers 1–6, circle the correct plural form of each noun in bold.

1. **calf**   calfs   calves

2. **man**   men   mans

3. **woman**   womans   women

4. **mouse**   mice   mouses

5. **loaf**   loafs   loaves

6. **knife**   knives   knifes

For Numbers 7–10, circle the correct plural noun in each sentence.

7. The (childs, children) walk to the store.

8. The (leafs, leaves) fell from the tree.

9. My (foots, feet) were hurting after I ran.

10. The horse's (hoofs, hooves) were sore after the race.

Minute 66

Name _____

For Numbers 1–5, circle the plural noun in each sentence.

1. The geese flew over our house.

2. There were a lot of people at the baseball game.

3. I have two shelves on my bedroom wall.

4. Be careful because the knives are very sharp!

5. We baked two loaves of bread for dinner.

For Numbers 6–10, write the correct plural form for the underlined noun in each sentence.

6. I lost two <u>tooth</u> last week.   _____

7. The three <u>man</u> built a fence.   _____

8. The <u>child</u> took a trip with their parents.   _____

9. Why are so many <u>person</u> here?   _____

10. All the <u>leaf</u> are red, yellow, and orange. _____

Grammar Minutes • Grade 2 © 2009 Creative Teaching Press

More Irregular Plural Nouns

Minute 67

Name _____

Answer the questions about *how, when,* or *where* something happens.

1. The deer quickly crossed the street.
How did the deer cross the street?_____

2. The little girl ate her food fast.
How did the little girl eat her food?_____

3. They found your house easily.
How did they find your house?_____

4. We will go camping tomorrow.
When will we go camping? _____

5. The Jones family went to the beach on Saturday.
When did the Jones family go to the beach?_____

6. My father and I flew our kites yesterday.
When did my father and I fly our kites? _____

7. The accident was near my house.
Where was the accident?_____

8. The dog slept outside.
Where did the dog sleep?_____

9. The airplane flew above our house.
Where did the plane fly?_____

10. The cat's toy rolled under the table.
Where did the cat's toy roll?_____

Grammar Minutes • Grade 2 © 2009 Creative Teaching Press

Minute 68

Name _____

For Numbers 1–6, use the adverbs in the box to complete the sentences below. Use each adverb only once.

(**Hint**: An *adverb* is a word that describes a verb and tells *how, when,* or *where* something happens.)

quickly	slowly	safely
carefully	sadly	neatly

1. The snail _____ crawled on the grass.

2. I _____ made up my bed.

3. We were _____ inside during the storm.

4. Jill drove _____ in the snow.

5. I _____ got ready for school this morning.

6. Kelly spoke _____ about her cat that died.

For Numbers 7–10, write whether the underlined adverb tells *how,* *when,* or *where* something happens in each sentence.

7. Kate and Sofia are going skating <u>tonight</u>.   _____

8. George <u>sadly</u> cried when he lost the game.   _____

9. Monica whispered <u>softly</u> into the telephone.   _____

10. The cat played <u>inside</u> the house.   _____

Grammar Minutes • Grade 2 © 2009 Creative Teaching Press

More Adverbs

Minute 69

Name _____

For Numbers 1–6, circle the correct verb in each sentence.

1. Marlon (brush, brushes) his teeth three times a day.

2. Dee (ate, eats) a sandwich for lunch yesterday.

3. The library (open, opens) at noon on Saturday.

4. Victor (rides, rode) his bike this morning.

5. The puppy (scratched, scratch) behind his ears.

6. I (wrote, writed) a poem for the talent show.

For Numbers 7–10, circle the correct noun in each sentence.

7. The three (boys, boy) are best friends.

8. An (apples, apple) is on the teacher's desk.

9. The (flower, flowers) smell sweet and fresh.

10. The (children, child) play after school.

Grammar Minutes • Grade 2 © 2009 Creative Teaching Press

Minute 70

Name _____

For Numbers 1–5, write *Yes* if the sentence is written correctly or *No* if it is not.

(**Hint**: The verb of the sentence must agree with the subject noun in number. For example: One *girl goes* to the store. Two *girls go* to the store.)

1. Fabian go fishing with his dad. _____

2. Sue listens to the birds chirp. _____

3. The mouse run from the cat. _____

4. The bookstore is closed. _____

5. Bianca eat a snack in the afternoon. _____

For Numbers 6–10, circle the correct noun and verb in each sentence.

6. The six (child, children) (play, plays) football.

7. A (chair, chairs) (fall, fell) on the floor.

8. The two (lady, ladies) (walk, walks) their dogs.

9. Please (wash, washes) all the (plates, plate).

10. The three (kid, kids) (helps, helped) their dad.

Grammar Minutes • Grade 2 © 2009 Creative Teaching Press

Minute 71

Name _____

Write *Yes* if the underlined article is used correctly or *No* if it is not.

1. The man climbed the tall mountain. _____

2. An frog jumped into the pond. _____

3. My dad's computer has a old keyboard. _____

4. Charlie is a only student who is absent. _____

5. Darla is eating a orange. _____

6. Chloe chose the red dress, not the blue one. _____

7. We had a picnic at an park. _____

8. Dustin is a friend of mine. _____

9. Lana had fun on the swings. _____

10. I ate a egg sandwich for breakfast. _____

Grammar Minutes • Grade 2 © 2009 Creative Teaching Press

Minute 72

Name _____

For Numbers 1–5, circle the correct verb to complete each sentence.

1. I (tore, tear) a hole in my favorite skirt.

2. Mandy (thinked, thought) she had another book to read.

3. Jasmine and her sister (swimmed, swam) in their pool.

4. Randi (freezed, froze) the water bottles.

5. The birds (flied, flew) to their new nest.

For Numbers 6–10, write the correct plural form for each noun.

6. mouse _____

7. foot _____

8. wolf _____

9. fish _____

10. deer _____

Grammar Minutes • Grade 2 © 2009 Creative Teaching Press

Irregular Verbs and Plural Nouns Review

Minute 73

Name _____

Circle the adverbs in the sentences below.
(**Hint**: Remember that *adverbs* tell *how, when,* or *where* something happens.)

1. The dog lazily walked into his doghouse.

2. May we go anywhere we want?

3. The music store moved closer to my house.

4. We made it safely to Memphis.

5. The cat drinks milk every day.

6. Carrie sat across from Nicki.

7. Marcia softly brushed the dog's fur.

8. He angrily told me no!

9. The girl neatly wrote the alphabet.

10. Sara can easily win the singing contest.

Minute 74

Name _____

Write *Yes* if the sentences are written correctly or *No* if they are not.

(**Hint**: Remember that the verb of the sentence must agree with the subject noun in number. For example: One *girl goes* to the store. Two *girls go* to the store.)

1. The growling dog scare me.   _____

2. My cat love to climb big trees.   _____

3. I swim in my neighbor's pool.   _____

4. The basket were too small for my flowers.   _____

5. They ride their bikes on the beach.   _____

6. I smells the paint in the room.   _____

7. The sour lemon tastes terrible.   _____

8. Michael are going to the dentist tomorrow.   _____

9. John run with his dad on the track.   _____

10. Today is a perfect day to go swimming.   _____

Grammar Minutes • Grade 2 © 2009 Creative Teaching Press

Noun and Verb Agreement Review

Minute 75

Name _____

For Numbers 1–4, write *C* if the sentence is complete or *I* if it is incomplete.

1. I eat a snack when I get home from school. _____

2. My favorite food. _____

3. Make sure to brush your teeth after each meal. _____

4. The sleeping dog. _____

For Numbers 5–7, write *Yes* if the sentences are in the correct word order or *No* if they are not.

5. Becky backyard in the played. _____

6. Went to the aquarium our class. _____

7. We are going to the movies. _____

For Numbers 8–10, circle the sentences that are written correctly.

8. **a.** officer george is the school guard.
    b. Officer George is the school guard.

9. **a.** Edwina's mom is from New York.
    b. Edwina's mom is from New york.

10. **a.** Dr. Jones is the principal at jackson Elementary.
    b. Dr. Jones is the principal at Jackson Elementary.

Grammar Minutes • Grade 2 © 2009 Creative Teaching Press

Minute 76

Name _____

Circle the words or groups of words that should begin with capital letters.
(**Hint**: There are two words or groups of words in each sentence to circle.)

1. jamie attends thomas jefferson Elementary.

2. her teacher's name is ms. rice.

3. cindy and marcia are Jan's best friends.

4. we had fun this summer at disney world.

5. my sister and i rode roller coasters.

6. my brother kyle liked the water rides.

7. next year my parents are taking us to sea world.

8. we sold lemonade on butler road.

9. my birthday is next tuesday.

10. mrs. turner picked allen to be the line leader.

Grammar Minutes • Grade 2 © 2009 Creative Teaching Press

Apply Your Grammar Knowledge

Minute 77

Name _____

For Numbers 1–5, add the correct end punctuation mark to each sentence.

1. What does this say_____

2. I had to clean my room before I could play_____

3. May we go to the beach today_____

4. Mrs. Todd taught a lesson on weather today_____

5. Don't ever do that again _____

For Numbers 6–10, read each sentence, and write the type of sentence it is on the line. Put *T* for telling, *A* for asking, or *E* for exclaiming.

6. How many apples are in the basket?   _____

7. I just won a new bicycle!   _____

8. My dad works at the post office.   _____

9. May we have one more minute to finish?   _____

10. The plane crashed into the mountain!   _____

Minute 78

Name _____

Circle two nouns and underline one verb in each sentence.

1. The firefighter saved the cat from the burning house.

2. The flowers need a lot of water and sunlight.

3. The dog got full of mud in the backyard.

4. The nurse put a bandage on my cut.

5. Greg washes his dog in the bathtub.

6. Tony sprays water on his sister.

7. The child ran out of the car and into the street.

8. My friends played games after school.

9. Susie read a lot of books during vacation.

10. My teacher graded my test this morning.

Grammar Minutes • Grade 2 © 2009 Creative Teaching Press

Apply Your Grammar Knowledge

Minute 79

Name _____

For Numbers 1–4, write the nouns in plural form.

1. girl _____

2. ditch _____

3. baby _____

4. mouse _____

For Numbers 5–10, circle the correct plural noun in each sentence.

5. There are five school (buses, busies) in the parking lot.

6. I have three older (sisteres, sisters).

7. Our dog had seven (puppys, puppies).

8. We took swim (classies, classes) this summer.

9. Yasmine takes her (boxs, boxes) of books to the car.

10. The (floweres, flowers) in Mrs. Paul's garden are now blooming.

Grammar Minutes • Grade 2 © 2009 Creative Teaching Press

Minute 80

Name _____

For Numbers 1–4, circle *Present* if the sentence is in the present tense or *Past* if it is in the past tense.

1. Serena gave Donna tennis lessons this morning. Present Past

2. James brought the sandwiches to the picnic. Present Past

3. The birds are in the sky. Present Past

4. We are celebrating Mindy's birthday. Present Past

For Numbers 5–10, write *Yes* if the sentence has the correct verb tense or *No* if it does not.

5. We jump in the pool yesterday. _____

6. The cats played on the table now. _____

7. I helped my mother clean the house last week. _____

8. She bump her elbow yesterday on the wall. _____

9. I learned how to count to 100 in kindergarten. _____

10. The turtle eats a fish ten minutes ago. _____

Grammar Minutes • Grade 2 © 2009 Creative Teaching Press

Apply Your Grammar Knowledge

Minute 81

Name _____

For Numbers 1–3, circle the adjective in each sentence.

1. I gave my mother red roses for Mother's Day.

2. The sad puppy was looking for a home.

3. The strong man saved us.

For Numbers 4–10, use the adjectives in the box to complete each sentence. Use each adjective only once.

bitter	sweet	fresh	purple
sour	spicy	handsome	

4. The chocolate cake was too _____.

5. I don't like lemons because they taste _____.

6. The _____ apple was not very good.

7. I burned my mouth eating the _____ chicken wings.

8. I think _____ grapes taste better than green grapes.

9. We bought _____ fruits and vegetables at the market.

10. The _____ man over there is my father.

Grammar Minutes • Grade 2 © 2009 Creative Teaching Press

Minute 82

Name _____

For Numbers 1–5, write *Yes* **if the underlined verb is used correctly or** *No* **if it is not.**

1. We <u>was</u> at school during the snowstorm.   _____

2. The dog <u>is</u> scared of the water.   _____

3. Nick <u>have</u> five dollars in his piggy bank.   _____

4. They <u>am</u> my cousins from Mexico.   _____

5. The field trip <u>is</u> tomorrow afternoon.   _____

For Numbers 6–10, circle the correct verb in each sentence.

6. I (is, am) the Student of the Month for April.

7. Math (is, are) one of my favorite subjects.

8. Mrs. Gomez (has, have) sixteen students in her class.

9. The horses (was, were) so gentle and beautiful.

10. Becky and I (is, are) both in karate classes.

Grammar Minutes • Grade 2 © 2009 Creative Teaching Press

Apply Your Grammar Knowledge

Minute 83

Name _____

For Numbers 1–5, write *Yes* if the commas are used correctly or *No* if they are not.

1. We will need glue, crayons, and scissors.   _____

2. Marie got, clothes, a watch and shoes.   _____

3. Joe's party will be on Sunday, August 15, 2010.   _____

4. We live at 1234, West Road Juniper, Florida.   _____

5. Tuesday, January 13, is when I broke my arm.   _____

For Numbers 6–10, circle the sentences that are written correctly.

6. **a.** Brian, Mike, and Chris are in a rock band.
    b. Brian, Mike, and, Chris are in a rock band.

7. **a.** My mother was born on February, 28 1975.
    b. My mother was born on February 28, 1975.

8. **a.** We are going to Paris, France, this summer.
    b. We are going to Paris France this summer.

9. **a.** My address is 4567 Hunter Way, Alphabet City.
    b. My address is 4567 Hunter Way Alphabet City.

10. **a.** I ate a hamburger, french fries and, an apple for lunch.
    b. I ate a hamburger, french fries, and an apple for lunch.

Grammar Minutes • Grade 2 © 2009 Creative Teaching Press

Minute 84

Name _____

Write *Yes* if the underlined pronoun in each sentence is correct or *No* if it is not.

1. Her made chicken salad and potatoes for us. _____

2. Me am not going to the dance with them. _____

3. Justin is mad because you told him to leave. _____

4. They went to Canada to visit their family. _____

5. Why does the puppy always follow us? _____

6. I will ask the teacher when I see she. _____

7. Mom and Dad will be happy if you help they. _____

8. Jessica's sister wants to play with her. _____

9. We only have one hour left in the library. _____

10. I am shopping for his birthday present today. _____

Grammar Minutes • Grade 2 © 2009 Creative Teaching Press

Apply Your Grammar Knowledge

Minute 85

Name _____

For Numbers 1–5, write the words that make up each contraction.

1. shouldn't _____ _____

2. don't _____ _____

3. won't _____ _____

4. she's _____ _____

5. didn't _____ _____

For Numbers 6–10, write a contraction to replace the underlined words.

6. <u>We will</u> go to the beach when it's hot. _____

7. The children <u>are not</u> going to the circus. _____

8. I <u>have not</u> seen his new car yet. _____

9. <u>She is</u> going to the store to buy ice cream. _____

10. Molly <u>can not</u> go to school because she is sick. _____

Grammar Minutes • Grade 2 © 2009 Creative Teaching Press

Minute 86

Name _____

For **Numbers 1–4**, circle the compound word in each sentence.

1. We found lots of seashells at the beach.

2. I put the letter in the mailbox.

3. My dog will not go into his doghouse.

4. My parents are painting my bedroom pink.

For **Numbers 5–10**, use the words in the box to write compound words on the lines below. Use each word only once.

back	rail	fast	knob
road	door	corn	sun
light	yard	break	pop

5. _____

6. _____

7. _____

8. _____

9. _____

10. _____

Apply Your Grammar Knowledge

Minute 87

Name _____

Write *S* if the pairs of words are synonyms (mean the same thing) or *A* if they are antonyms (mean the opposite).

1. race   run   _____

2. wrong   right   _____

3. thin   thick   _____

4. bright   smart   _____

5. happy   cheerful   _____

6. no one   everyone   _____

7. funny   silly   _____

8. early   late   _____

9. sleep   rest   _____

10. open   close   _____

Grammar Minutes • Grade 2 © 2009 Creative Teaching Press

Minute 88

Name _____

For Numbers 1–5, circle the correct meaning for each underlined word.

1. The dog bite on my leg is very <u>painful</u>.
   a. full of pain   **b.** one who is in pain

2. We learned what <u>uneven</u> numbers are in math class.
   a. even again   **b.** not even

3. The <u>dancer</u> got a new pair of ballet slippers.
   a. dance again   **b.** a person who dances

4. I have to <u>rewrite</u> my messy homework.
   a. write again   **b.** full of writing

5. The baby's birth was a <u>joyful</u> event.
   a. one who has joy   **b.** full of joy

For Numbers 6–10, use the words in the box to best complete the story.

| disappears | reappears | quickly | magical | helper |

Paul the Great is our classroom magician. The tricks he can do are truly

6. _____! One minute he has a rabbit in his hat, and then it

suddenly **7.** _____ into thin air. When Paul the Great taps

the hat again, the rabbit **8.** _____. When I was his magician's

9. _____, I tried to learn all his tricks. Paul the Great does his

tricks too **10.** _____ for anyone to learn them.

Grammar Minutes • Grade 2 © 2009 Creative Teaching Press

Apply Your Grammar Knowledge

Minute 89

Name _____

For Numbers 1–6, write the words in the box in ABC order.

shells	water	umbrella
beach	sand	towel

1. _____

2. _____

3. _____

4. _____

5. _____

6. _____

For Numbers 7–10, write each set of words in ABC order.

7. blue, black, bleed _____

8. champ, cheap, chirp _____

9. stripe, struck, strong _____

10. breathe, brain, bring _____

Grammar Minutes • Grade 2 © 2009 Creative Teaching Press

Minute 90

Name _____

For Numbers 1–5, write each underlined noun as a possessive noun.

1. <u>Kaila</u> backpack is pink and green.   _____

2. The <u>boy</u> math project is almost done.   _____

3. <u>Amy</u> favorite watch is on the desk.   _____

4. The <u>baby</u> parents are taking her to
the zoo.   _____

5. <u>Ryan</u> winter vacation was fun.   _____

For Numbers 6–10, circle the correct possessive noun in each sentence.

6. The (cakes, cake's) frosting is melting in the sun.

7. The (pianos, piano's) color is a dark brown.

8. The (cars, car's) brakes need to be checked.

9. (Brenda's , Brenda) keys are locked in the car.

10. The little (girl, girl's) ballet slippers were too small.

Apply Your Grammar Knowledge

Minute 91

Name _____

Circle the correct article in each sentence.

1. I am eating (a, an, the) slice of cheese pizza.

2. (A, An, The) clock on the wall stopped.

3. We saw (a, an, the) elephant and a tiger at the zoo.

4. Tina wishes she had (a, an, the) little sister or brother.

5. (A, An, The) apple a day is good for your body.

6. Jarvis ate all of (a, an, the) pumpkin pie.

7. I like (a, an, the) new teacher we have this year.

8. Don's math test lasted (a, an, the) hour.

9. Did you know that (a, an, the) dog could live 20 years?

10. We saw (a, an, the) ostrich at the city zoo.

Grammar Minutes • Grade 2 © 2009 Creative Teaching Press

Minute 92

Name _____

Circle the correct word in each sentence.

1. Tommy (leaved, left) his baseball glove at home.

2. The track team (ran, runned) a mile for practice.

3. The (goose, geese) fly south for the winter.

4. Those shoes are too small for my (feet, foot).

5. The (person, people) are talking too loudly.

6. The birds (fly, flies) high up in the sky.

7. Bobby (watches, watch) his dad fix the car.

8. The man is cutting (a, an) branch off of the tree.

9. Steve (was, were) the first person to get to school.

10. (We, us) are going to the park to play soccer.

Grammar Minutes • Grade 2 © 2009 Creative Teaching Press

Apply Your Grammar Knowledge

Minute 93

Name _____

Circle the incorrect word in each sentence, and write it correctly on the line.

1. The puppys are fighting over the bone.   _____

2. Mike was'nt happy with his grades.   _____

3. My mom is taking we to the movies.   _____

4. I is going to make pancakes for breakfast.   _____

5. Mrs. watson was my first-grade teacher.   _____

6. Lena go to dance practice every day.   _____

7. We live on 789 Crest Drive in San francisco.   _____

8. Thomas are outside playing with his neighbor.   _____

9. The boys looked for their cat fluffy all day.   _____

10. Samantha can read much fast than I can.   _____

Grammar Minutes • Grade 2 © 2009 Creative Teaching Press

Minute 94

Name _____

For Numbers 1–4, circle the incorrect words in each sentence, and then write the entire sentence correctly on the line.
(**Hint**: Each sentence has two incorrect words or groups of words.)

1. Mr. smith came home with two puppys for his kids.

_____

2. They is going to disney world for a week.

_____

3. mrs. Smith wants to shop in the many store.

_____

4. Mr. Smith and reggie Jr. want to rides all of the roller coasters.

_____

For Numbers 5–10, circle the correct word in each sentence.

5. Patty and Lauren (want, wants) to see a movie.

6. They are looking forward to their first (plane, plain) ride.

7. Please raise your (right, write) hand.

8. The dog (runned, ran) around the tree.

9. I (couldn't, coulnd't) decide whether or not to order cake or pie.

10. (She, Her) mother is taking us to the movies after school.

Grammar Minutes • Grade 2 © 2009 Creative Teaching Press

Apply Your Grammar Knowledge

Minute 95

Name _____

Read the story, and circle the 10 words that are incorrect. Write them correctly on the lines below.

Today in class us learned that a verb is a action word. Mrs. thompson ask

each student to pull an action word out of a hat and act it out in front of the

class. sallys word were dance. She done a ballet step she learned in

ballet class. My word was clap. The students guessed my action write away.

My best friend, john, skipped around the room. everyone was laughing. We

had fun acting out our action words.

1. _____   6. _____

2. _____   7. _____

3. _____   8. _____

4. _____   9. _____

5. _____   10. _____

Grammar Minutes • Grade 2 © 2009 Creative Teaching Press

Minute 96

Name _____

For Numbers 1–3, rewrite the sentences in the correct word order.

1. Loudly barked at the man the dog.

_____

2. The boy quickly up the stairs ran.

_____

3. Toward prey tiger the moved slowly its.

_____

For Numbers 4–10, circle the incorrect word in each sentence, and write it correctly on the line.

4. There was'n't any bread left to make
a sandwich.   _____

5. Tosha loves to swam in the pool.   _____

6. Cassie cant reach the cookie jar.   _____

7. I eight peach pie for dessert.   _____

8. The wind blue my hat away.   _____

9. Them are coming to the library with us.   _____

10. I are working hard on my math test.   _____

Apply Your Grammar Knowledge

Minute 97

Name _____

Write *N* if the sentence is missing a noun or *V* if it is missing a verb.
(**Hint**: Write a word to complete each sentence. Then see if it is a noun or a verb.)

1. My teacher _____ around the room. _____

2. I had fun eating lunch with my _____ today. _____

3. The dog was covered in _____ after the rain. _____

4. The party _____ is now too small for her to wear. _____

5. We had fun _____ in the rain yesterday. _____

6. Martin and _____ take their dog to the vet. _____

7. I _____ up my bed every morning before school. _____

8. The fluffy clouds _____ so high in the sky. _____

9. Many _____ were at the parade. _____

10. Chelsea _____ every Saturday morning. _____

Grammar Minutes • Grade 2 © 2009 Creative Teaching Press

Minute 98

Name _____

For Numbers 1–3, circle two nouns and underline one verb in each sentence.

1. The girls often play in the park.

2. Jazmine always does her homework.

3. Sometimes, Jalen eats a whole hamburger.

For Numbers 4–10, circle the sentences that are written correctly.

4. a. Tyler loves to go to his grandparents' home.
   b. tyler loves to go to his grandparents' home.

5. a. They have a big apple tree in the backyard.
   b. Them have a big apple tree in the backyard.

6. a. We have ate new students this year.
   b. We have eight new students this year.

7. a. Olivia is the cuter puppy at the dog show.
   b. Olivia is the cutest puppy at the dog show.

8. a. Joey often climbs to the top of the tree in his yard.
   b. Joey often climb to the top of the tree in his yard.

9. a. Maria asked her parents if she could go with they.
   b. Maria asked her parents if she could go with them.

10. a. Those men are helping my mother with the car.
    b. Those mans are helping my mother with the car.

Apply Your Grammar Knowledge

Minute 99

Name _____

Write the correct present- and past-tense form in each sentence.

Present Tense	Past Tense

1. She _____
             wrote writes
 on the board.
	2. I _____ my
	            wrote writes
	 grandma a letter.

3. My dad is _____
             flew flying
 that plane.
	4. The bird _____
	             flew flying
	 into the window.

5. I _____ too
        speak spoke
 loudly sometimes.
	6. A famous artist
	
	 _____ at
	        speak spoke
	 my school.

7. Paul _____
        throws threw
 the trash away for his mom.
	8. He _____
	        throws threw
	 my favorite toy in the pool!

9. Julio is _____
        read reading
 the newspaper.
	10. I _____ a
	        read reading
	 funny story yesterday.

Grammar Minutes • Grade 2 © 2009 Creative Teaching Press

Minute 100

Name _____

For Numbers 1–5, circle the adjectives in the sentences.
(**Hint**: Each sentence has two adjectives to circle.)

1. The bright students solved the difficult problem.

2. My favorite cousins live in sunny Florida.

3. The gray dog loves his caring family.

4. I am going to wear my new pink dress on Sunday.

5. I have twelve red roses to give to you.

For Numbers 6–10, circle the incorrect word in each sentence, and then write it correctly on the line.

6. I doesn't have any money for lunch. _____

7. Why are he going to the office? _____

8. Regina dropped the book on she foot. _____

9. Me can't roller-skate very well. _____

10. Carrie luggage was lost at the airport. _____

Grammar Minutes • Grade 2 © 2009 Creative Teaching Press

Apply Your Grammar Knowledge

Minute Answer Key

Minute 1
1. b
2. a
3. b
4. a
5. Complete
6. Incomplete
7. Complete
8. Complete
9. Incomplete
10. Complete

Minute 2
1. b
2. a
3. a
4. b
5. a
6. The movie was funny.
7. I ride on my bike.
8. The cat sleeps a lot.
9. The candy is sweet.
10. The puppy was lost.

Minute 3
1. A
2. T
3. E
4. A
5. T
6. T
7. A
8. E
9. T
10. T

Minute 4
1. b
2. a
3. a
4. a
5. b
6. b
7. b
8. a
9. a
10. b

Minute 5
1. I
2. We
3. Sarah's
4. Wednesday
5. My
6. April
7. Max
8. California
9. They
10. Every

Minute 6
1. ?
2. !
3. !
4. .
5. .
6. ?
7. !
8. .
9. .
10. ?

Minute 7
Order of answers may vary.
1. student
2. sister
3. teacher
4. coach
5. park
6. school
7. lake
8. phone
9. flower
10. radio

Minute 8
1. girls, park
2. Brandon, books
3. Apples, grapes
4. Marie, Tina
5. Tom, cake
6. beach, summer
7. Chris, dog
8. dog, cat
9. clouds, sky
10. Mr. Manson, teacher

Minute 9
1. Meg, Amy
2. Charlie
3. Nick, Mitch
4. Lucky
5. Punka
6. Timothy
7. Nicole
8. Megan, Madison
9. Mozart
10. Bubbles

Minute 10
1. b
2. a
3. b
4. a
5. b
6. a
7. b
8. a
9. a
10. b

Minute 11
1. Uncle Herbert
2. Dr. Dawson
3. Mrs. Gomez
4. Police Officer Edwards
5. Grandma Rose
6. c
7. a
8. b
9. c
10. b

Minute 12
1. Washington Elementary School
2. Parker Garden Center
3. Burger Express
4. Doggie Kennel
5. Chicago, Illinois
6. Rose Park
7. Bouldercrest Mall
8. Florida
9. Smith Library
10. Jackson Street

Minute 13
1. C
2. I
3. C
4. a
5. b
6. T
7. E
8. A
9. E
10. A

Minute 14
1. How are you?
2. My desk is dirty.
3. The clock is black.
4. Wow, she's tall!
5. I play the piano.
6. No
7. No
8. Yes
9. Yes
10. No

Minute 15
Order of answers for 1.–6. may vary.
1. principal
2. singer
3. hospital
4. bedroom
5. ring
6. brush
7. firefighter, kitten
8. flowers, garden
9. dog, toy
10. nurse, cut

Minute 16
1. Thomas
2. Lincoln
3. Seattle
4. Washington
5. Atlanta
6. Johnny's
7. Greene
8. Chi
9. Hua
10. Jennifer

Minute 17
The following 10 words should be circled:
1. chew
2. swim
3. clap
4. type
5. dance
6. smell
7. walk
8. eat
9. jump
10. drive

Minute 18
1. feeds
2. barks
3. play
4. reads
5. walked
6. swam
7. slides
8. rode
9. chirp
10. types

Minute 19
1. jogged
2. played
3. helps
4. have
5. was
6. danced
7. cried
8. licks
9. pulls
10. chews

Minute 20
1. scratches
2. scratched
3. yawn
4. yawned
5. write
6. wrote
7. is
8. raked
9. look
10. pitched

Minute Answer Key

Minute 21
1. is
2. are
3. am
4. is
5. is
6. is
7. is
8. am
9. are
10. is

Minute 22
1. was
2. was
3. were
4. was
5. were
6. was
7. were
8. was
9. were
10. was

Minute 23
1. have
2. has
3. have or had
4. have
5. has or had
6. have
7. has
8. had
9. had
10. have

Minute 24
1. gray
2. sweet
3. five
4. pretty
5. sour
6. tiny
7. green
8. loud
9. mean
10. little

Minute 25
1. taller
2. fastest
3. slowest
4. shorter
5. brighter
6. smartest
7. nicest
8. bigger
9. cleaner
10. deepest

Minute 26
1. Glendale, Arizona
2. Columbus, Ohio
3. Paris, France
4. Ivy Lane, Washington
5. Peachtree Street, Ashton
6. June 30, 1987
7. August 1, 2009
8. Monday, August
9. June 30, 2010
10. May 10, 2008

Minute 27
1. read, skate
2. soccer, and
3. candy, popcorn
4. lions, tigers
5. b
6. a
7. b
8. b
9. a
10. b

Minute 28
The following 10 words should be circled:
1. went
2. saw
3. drew
4. told
5. run
6. play
7. ate
8. rode
9. write
10. read

Minute 29
1. No
2. Yes
3. No
4. Past
5. Present
6. Present
7. Past
8. was
9. is
10. had

Minute 30
1. smart
2. fastest
3. red
4. fresh
5. yellow
6. prettiest
7. beautiful
8. healthier
9. best
10. longer

Minute 31
1. pancakes, eggs
2. Austin, Texas
3. July 4, 2008
4. b
5. a
6. b
7. No
8. Yes
9. Yes
10. No

Minute 32
1. I
2. me
3. me
4. I
5. me
6. me
7. I
8. I
9. me
10. me

Minute 33
1. No
2. Yes
3. No
4. No
5. Yes
6. He
7. She
8. her
9. him
10. She

Minute 34
1. We
2. us
3. We
4. us
5. We
6. We
7. us
8. we
9. We
10. us

Minute 35
1. They
2. them
3. They
4. They
5. them
6. No
7. Yes
8. Yes
9. Yes
10. No

Minute 36
1. dresses
2. cats
3. girls
4. beaches
5. foxes
6. ponies
7. friends
8. toys
9. brothers
10. cities

Minute 37
1. ponies
2. babies
3. trucks
4. foxes
5. glasses
6. pencils
7. apples
8. boxes
9. boys
10. classes

Minute 38
1. baby's
2. Nicole's
3. painter's
4. clock's
5. city's
6. a giraffe's neck
7. the dog's mat
8. the turtle's shell
9. the car's tires
10. Ming's dress

Minute 39
1. Don't
2. I'm
3. can't
4. haven't
5. shouldn't
6. No
7. Yes
8. No
9. Yes
10. Yes

Minute 40
1. haven't
2. wasn't
3. She's
4. I'll
5. didn't
6. can not
7. is not
8. do not
9. has not
10. should not

Minute Answer Key

Minute 41
1. doghouse
2. raincoat
3. sunglasses
4. newspaper
5–10. afternoon, toothpaste, classroom, watermelon, grandfather, homework

Minute 42
1. backyard
2. outside
3. playground
4. basketball
5. Yes
6. No
7. No
8. Yes
9. Yes
10. No

Minute 43
1. She
2. They
3. him
4. He
5. She
6. us
7. He
8. They
9. her
10. I

Minute 44
1. carrots
2. families
3. couches
4. classes
5. axes
6. dog's
7. cake's
8. children's
9. chair's
10. computer's

Minute 45
1. he's
2. doesn't
3. aren't
4. you're
5. you'll
6. would have
7. will not
8. is not
9. did not
10. must not

Minute 46
1. skyscrapers
2. earthworm
3. peppermints
4. snowman
5. wristwatch
6. sunflowers
7. birdhouse
8. postcard
9. rattlesnake
10. homework

Minute 47
1. angry
2. scream
3. beautiful
4. hop
5. sleepy
6. small
7. hates
8. buddy
9. unhappy
10. completed

Minute 48
1. quiet, silent
2. old, ancient
3. talk, speak
4. rich, wealthy
5. No
6. No
7. No
8. No
9. Yes
10. Yes

Minute 49
1. go
2. up
3. sit
4. asleep
5. forget
6. run
7. dull
8. quiet
9. huge
10. neat

Minute 50
1. late
2. hot
3. right
4. terrible
5. dry
6. pretty
7. down
8. fast
9. small or little
10. low

Minute 51
1. sun
2. see
3. piece
4. prey
5. bee
6. blue
7. Yes
8. No
9. Yes
10. No

Minute 52
1. b
2. a
3. b
4. b
5. a
6. b
7. c
8. d
9. b
10. a

Minute 53
1. unhappy
2. rewrite
3. unhealthy
4. refill
5. unlucky
6. c
7. d
8. a
9. e
10. b

Minute 54
1. helper
2. hurtful
3. player
4. helpful
5. playful
6. painter: one who paints
7. colorful: full of color
8. cheerful: full of cheer
9. teacher: one who teaches
10. hopeful: full of hope

Minute 55
1. duck
2. five
3. grapes
4. job
5. skate
6. weather
7. Yes
8. Yes
9. No
10. Yes

Minute 56
1. shake, slide, snap
2. already, any, apple
3. grape, great, grew
4. draw, drink, drum
5. handsome
6. head
7. heat
8. home
9. house
10. hum

Minute 57
1. S
2. A
3. A
4. S
5. A
6. S
7. A
8. S
9. A
10. S

Minute 58
1. sun
2. made
3. plane
4. meet
5. write
6. hi
7. c
8. a
9. d
10. b

Minute 59
1. S
2. P
3. S
4. S
5. P
6. replay
7. driver
8. unpack
9. beautiful
10. reread

Minute 60
1. No
2. Yes
3. Yes
4. No
5. Yes
6. No
7. Yes
8. Yes
9. No
10. Yes

Minute Answer Key

Minute 61
1. an
2. a
3. a
4. An
5. a
6. a
7. an
8. a
9. an
10. a

Minute 62
1. the
2. a
3. The
4. an or the
5. a
6. the
7. a
8. the
9. the
10. An

Minute 63
1. fed
2. threw
3. wrote
4. made
5. took
6. ran
7. froze
8. stood
9. left
10. read

Minute 64
1. hold
2. take
3. catch
4. fight
5. wear
6. run
7. took
8. grew
9. swam
10. sold

Minute 65
1. calves
2. men
3. women
4. mice
5. loaves
6. knives
7. children
8. leaves
9. feet
10. hooves

Minute 66
1. geese
2. people
3. shelves
4. knives
5. loaves
6. teeth
7. men
8. children
9. people
10. leaves

Minute 67
1. quickly
2. fast
3. easily
4. tomorrow
5. on Saturday
6. yesterday
7. near my house
8. outside
9. above our house
10. under the table

Minute 68
1. slowly
2. neatly
3. safely
4. carefully
5. quickly
6. sadly
7. when
8. how
9. how
10. where

Minute 69
1. brushes
2. ate
3. opens
4. rode
5. scratched
6. wrote
7. boys
8. apple
9. flowers
10. children

Minute 70
1. No
2. Yes
3. No
4. Yes
5. No
6. children, play
7. chair, fell
8. ladies, walk
9. wash, plates
10. kids, helped

Minute 71
1. Yes
2. No
3. No
4. No
5. No
6. Yes
7. No
8. Yes
9. Yes
10. No

Minute 72
1. tore
2. thought
3. swam
4. froze
5. flew
6. mice
7. feet
8. wolves
9. fish
10. deer

Minute 73
1. lazily
2. anywhere
3. closer
4. safely
5. every day
6. across
7. softly
8. angrily
9. neatly
10. easily

Minute 74
1. No
2. No
3. Yes
4. No
5. Yes
6. No
7. Yes
8. No
9. No
10. Yes

Minute 75
1. C
2. I
3. C
4. I
5. No
6. No
7. Yes
8. b
9. a
10. b

Minute 76
1. Jamie, Thomas Jefferson
2. Her, Ms. Rice
3. Cindy, Marcia
4. We, Disney World
5. My, I
6. My, Kyle
7. Next, Sea World
8. We, Butler Road
9. My, Tuesday
10. Mrs. Turner, Allen

Minute 77
1. ?
2. .
3. ?
4. .
5. !
6. A
7. E
8. T
9. A
10. E

Minute 78
Possible answers include:
1. Nouns: firefighter, cat, house
   Verb: saved
2. Nouns: flowers, water, sunlight
   Verb: need
3. Nouns: dog, mud, backyard
   Verb: got
4. Nouns: nurse, bandage, cut
   Verb: put
5. Nouns: Greg, dog, bathtub
   Verb: washes
6. Nouns: Tony, water, sister
   Verb: sprays
7. Nouns: child, car, street
   Verb: ran
8. Nouns: friends, games, school
   Verb: played
9. Nouns: Susie, books, vacation
   Verb: read
10. Nouns: teacher, test, morning
    Verb: graded

Minute Answer Key

Minute 79
1. girls
2. ditches
3. babies
4. mice
5. buses
6. sisters
7. puppies
8. classes
9. boxes
10. flowers

Minute 80
1. Past
2. Past
3. Present
4. Present
5. No
6. No
7. Yes
8. No
9. Yes
10. No

Minute 81
1. red
2. sad
3. strong
4. sweet
5. sour
6. bitter
7. spicy
8. purple
9. fresh
10. handsome

Minute 82
1. No
2. Yes
3. No
4. No
5. Yes
6. am
7. is
8. has
9. were
10. are

Minute 83
1. Yes
2. No
3. Yes
4. No
5. Yes
6. a
7. b
8. a
9. a
10. b

Minute 84
1. No
2. No
3. Yes
4. Yes
5. Yes
6. No
7. No
8. Yes
9. Yes
10. Yes

Minute 85
1. should not
2. do not
3. will not
4. she is
5. did not
6. We'll
7. aren't
8. haven't
9. She's
10. can't

Minute 86
1. seashells
2. mailbox
3. doghouse
4. bedroom
5–10. backyard, railroad, sunlight, popcorn, doorknob, breakfast

Minute 87
1. S
2. A
3. A
4. S
5. S
6. A
7. S
8. A
9. S
10. A

Minute 88
1. a
2. b
3. b
4. a
5. b
6. magical
7. disappears
8. reappears
9. helper
10. quickly

Minute 89
1. beach
2. sand
3. shells
4. towel
5. umbrella
6. water
7. black, bleed, blue
8. champ, cheap, chirp
9. stripe, strong, struck
10. brain, breathe, bring

Minute 90
1. Kaila's
2. boy's
3. Amy's
4. baby's
5. Ryan's
6. cake's
7. piano's
8. car's
9. Brenda's
10. girl's

Minute 91
1. a or the
2. The
3. an
4. a
5. An
6. the
7. the
8. an
9. a
10. an

Minute 92
1. left
2. ran
3. geese
4. feet
5. people
6. fly
7. watches
8. a
9. was
10. We

Minute 93
1. puppies
2. wasn't
3. us
4. am
5. Watson
6. goes
7. Francisco
8. is
9. Fluffy
10. faster

Minute 94
1. Smith, puppies
2. are, Disney World
3. Mrs., stores
4. Reggie, ride
5. want
6. plane
7. right
8. ran
9. couldn't
10. Her

Minute 95
1. we
2. an
3. Thompson
4. asked
5. Sally's
6. was
7. did
8. right
9. John
10. Everyone

Minute 96
1. The dog barked loudly at the man. OR The dog loudly barked at the man.
2. The boy ran quickly up the stairs. OR The boy quickly ran up the stairs.
3. The tiger moved slowly toward its prey. OR The tiger slowly moved toward its prey.
4. wasn't
5. swim
6. can't
7. ate
8. blew
9. They
10. am

Minute 97
1. V
2. N
3. N
4. N
5. V
6. N
7. V
8. V
9. N
10. V

Minute 98
1. Nouns: girls, park
   Verb: play
2. Nouns: Jazmine, homework
   Verb: does
3. Nouns: Jalen, hamburger
   Verb: eats
4. a
5. a
6. b
7. b
8. a
9. b
10. a

Minute 99
1. writes
2. wrote
3. flying
4. flew
5. speak
6. spoke
7. throws
8. threw
9. reading
10. read

Minute 100
1. bright, difficult
2. favorite, sunny
3. gray, caring
4. new, pink
5. twelve, red
6. don't
7. is
8. her
9. I
10. Carrie's